INSTRUCTOR'S MANUAL

to accompany

The Practical Writer
6th edition

and

The Practical Writer With Readings
4th edition

Edward P. Bailey   Philip A. Powell

Harcourt Brace College Publishers

Fort Worth Philadelphia San Diego New York Orlando Austin San Antonio
Toronto Montreal London Sydney Tokyo

Address editorial correspondence to:
Harcourt Brace College Publishers
301 Commerce Street, Suite 3700
Fort Worth, TX 76102

Address orders to:
Harcourt Brace & Company
6277 Sea Harbor Drive
Orlando, FL 32887
1-800-782-4479 outside Florida
1-800-433-0001 inside Florida

ISBN: 0-15-5017896

Printed in the United States of America

4 5 6 7 8 9 0 1 2 3 023 10 9 8 7 6 5 4 3 2 1

Contents

1. Using *The Practical Writer*

This book has three major sections:

- *Section One, "A Model for Writing."* This section starts with a simple single paragraph, moves to a more complex single paragraph, and then to a simple essay.

- *Section Two, "Beyond the Model Essay."* Unlike Section One—which emphasizes tightly structured models—this section works more loosely with the organization of the essay to teach four common patterns of development and to present a short, simple research paper. Together, then, Sections One and Two move the student from a simple paragraph to a research paper.

- *Section Three, "Improving Your Punctuation and Expression."* Chapters in this section discuss common problems students have with usage and punctuation. The section will work as a block—that is, students can move through it one chapter after another—but you can also spread the chapters throughout a composition course or use them for reference as problems arise in a student's writing.

Here's a little more about each section of the book.

SECTION ONE

The key to Section One, containing Parts One to Three, is simplicity.

Part One presents what we call the "Stage I" one-paragraph essay: a single paragraph with a topic sentence, support, and a restated topic sentence. This short essay has the general form of a fuller one, but it's short enough to allow the students to concentrate on the fundamental problems of presenting an idea in writing. Chapters 1 to 5 of Part One present the form of the Stage I model, discussion of support, the topic sentence, unity, and coherence. We encourage students to write from their experiences or their imaginations because we're less interested at this point in depth of thought than in principles of composition. Students should learn what relevant and adequate supports are and how to direct those supports to persuade a reader to accept the topic idea. If students grasp these principles and can apply them to a simple paragraph essay, they'll be able to apply them later to more sophisticated topics.

Part Two then presents the Stage II one-paragraph essay. Here we retain the simplicity of the single paragraph but begin to break the topic idea into subtopic ideas. From here, it's an easy step to the simple theme, the five-paragraph essay.

Part Three, which presents the five-paragraph essay, explains the relationships between the topic sentence of the one-paragraph essay and the thesis statement of the five-paragraph essay, and between support for a one-paragraph essay and support for the five-paragraph essay. Chapters here also discuss two new types of paragraph—the introduction and the conclusion.

Throughout Section One, we present sample essays that students can easily imitate. We also present exercises that should help the students develop the skills they need for more complex writing.

SECTION TWO

Section Two—containing Parts Four and Five—retains the models students learned earlier in the book but suggests more flexibility.

Part Four discusses four ways to develop thesis statements:

- comparison and contrast

- cause and effect

- classification

- description of a process

Subjects become a little more sophisticated, but samples are still within the abilities of the students. Exercises emphasize the principle development pattern but encourage variation from the models we present.

Part Five completes the building process begun with the single paragraph by presenting the research paper. Besides discussing the model for a research paper, this part also takes the students step by step through the process of writing one—from finding support to documenting it in the final paper.

SECTION THREE

Section Three—containing Parts Six and Seven—deals with common punctuation and expression (including usage) problems in student writing. The section is not a comprehensive handbook; instead, chapters discuss punctuation, grammar, and expression problems that are often most troublesome for first-year college students.

2. General Teaching Techniques

By the time they reach your class, your students certainly have seen a great deal of writing and have developed some writing skills. But their knowledge is usually incomplete, their skills only partially developed. They can learn quickly, but they need straightforward instruction.

Let's say you want to teach a group of people how to change a tire. You can sit back and tell them how, but they may have trouble if they've never seen anyone do it. You could demonstrate changing a tire in front of them. Or you could supervise while they practice changing tires. The last choice probably is the best one. If they're worried about jumping right in, combining all three methods, and emphasizing the third, most likely will work. In other words, briefly tell them how to change a tire, demonstrate, and supervise practice. By the time you're through, your students will have developed a skill they can apply when you're no longer around to help.

We suggest you use the same approach in a class on composition. Spend a little time, of course, explaining the material in the day's lesson from *The Practical Writer*. We've found that although the book is simple, you need to reinforce the lesson; students tend to apply only the parts of the lesson that you discuss in class. Spend more time showing your students examples, perhaps ours or perhaps some that you bring in. And spend even more time letting your students show you that they understand the material. The more actively the students are involved in the writing process, the better they'll learn it.

Here are four other tips you might consider:

HAVE YOUR STUDENTS READ THEIR PAPERS ALOUD—IN CLASS

This is, perhaps, the most important advice we can give you. Remember when you were in college and you handed in a paper? There, on the instructor's desk, was a stack of everybody's work, and surely you wondered (as we did) just what the other students were doing. The best way to let your students know is to have a few students actually read their papers to the class the day papers are due.

The advantages? Many:

- First, reading aloud helps students to become acquainted with the work of their classmates—which can provide many more models, good and bad, for them to consider.

- Second, since the best writing sounds like good talking, reading aloud helps students tap into their own spoken language. Now, we know that many of our students are not entirely fluent when speaking, but when they think about writing the way they talk, somehow their writing improves dramatically: "writing the way you talk" is more metaphor than reality, but the advice works!

- Third, reading aloud helps the students create a real audience—the class—for their writing. After a few sessions of reading aloud, the students will begin to think they're writing for the class, for a real audience, instead of just for you as an "unreal audience" and an evaluator.

- Finally, when students become aware they may be reading their papers to the class, they'll often show a genuine concern for doing their best work.

Now—how to conduct the class when students read aloud? We suggest you concentrate on the larger levels of writing—the effectiveness of the support, the organization—than on matters such as grammar and usage. And, more important, keep your comments in class positive. Talk about what the students have done well, not what they've done badly. The value of the positive approach will come home if you and your colleagues do some writing and reading aloud to each other. The psychological damage from a careless, negative comment, in front of the other students, can be terminal. So be positive in class—you can make the necessary criticisms in writing when you comment on the paper itself.

LET YOUR STUDENTS REWRITE ONE PAPER

Normally, we don't announce this policy at the beginning of class. But as the semester goes along, students sometimes have trouble on a paper and revising it would be more valuable than going directly to the next assignment. So we give them some general guidance, a reasonable deadline, and a second chance. Almost always, the students work very hard on the rewrite to make the changes we suggest. And they almost always are far better prepared to move onto the next material in the course.

HAVE YOUR STUDENTS WRITE FREQUENTLY

The one-paragraph essay in Parts One and Two of *The Practical Writer* makes frequent writing less painful for the students than struggling with a full-length essay—and less painful for you because it's easy to evaluate. Still, if you're like us, you have plenty to evaluate. Fortunately, there's a way to work around this problem occasionally.

Divide your class into groups of three (if groups are larger, some students will remain spectators), assign a topic sentence, and give your students about thirty minutes to write a paragraph. Allow them to invent evidence, of course, and encourage them to be as imaginative as possible without lapsing into nonsense. You'll be surprised at how clever they can be and how well they can write as a group.

While the students are working, walk from group to group and help them out. Then, when time is up, have one member from each group read the group's paragraph to the class. If you've assigned the same topic to all groups, everyone will be interested in seeing what the other groups have done.

An important advantage for you is that you don't have to grade these paragraphs because you critique them orally in class. And as long as you tell the students that they'll be reading their paragraphs aloud, you won't need a grade to motivate them. Peer pressure will take care of that. Besides, the exercise is fun—for them and for you. Use it two or three times a term, especially early in the course.

FREQUENTLY TALK TO YOUR STUDENTS INDIVIDUALLY ABOUT THEIR WRITING

The one-on-one conference is perhaps the best technique for teaching writing because it lets you communicate clearly your response to the student's writing.

Use the conference at the expense of something else, if necessary. You can have conferences either outside class time or during a class workshop while the other students are working on an exercise, such as the group-writing activity.

One excellent occasion for running in-class conferences comes the day you return papers. Take a minute or two per student as you hand back papers individually. Don't try to cover every mistake, but do cover both what is particularly good and what you'd like to see improved on the next assignment. You'll be surprised how effective a friendly (or disappointed) look and a few spoken words can be. Looking a student in the eye as you caution him or her to use detailed support in the next essay will make your point far better than writing the same words at the bottom of the page.

Still, the most effective conferences are in your office when you can examine the last paper in detail and perhaps talk about ideas for the next one. We've found these conferences so useful that we occasionally excuse students from a class meeting to compensate them (and us) for the time we need to meet with them in the office.

In addition, we've discovered a technique for experienced instructors that can make these conferences even better. Read through the papers in advance, but don't mark on them. Then when the student comes in, read through the paper out loud (if it's a short one) and critique it (don't forget the good points!) as you go along. Not only does this keep the students from being defensive from the beginning (which they may well be if they've seen a grade on the paper), but it lets them find out exactly what you think about their writing. Written comments don't come close to communicating as well.

Once you've read through the entire paper, ask the student to help list the paper's strengths and weaknesses. Then ask the students what the grade ought to be. By that time, it's usually obvious to both of you. As the student gets ready to leave, mention the strengths you'd like to see repeated on the next paper and the recommendations you have for improvement.

If you haven't used the one-on-one conferences before, we think you'll be pleased at how effective they are. They have another positive effect: the personal (individual) contact with your students will really help with your rapport with the class as a whole.

3. A Word About Exercise Answers

Almost all the exercises in the first two sections of *The Practical Writer* require subjective responses from the students and, of course, subjective evaluation from you. Seldom, then, are there necessarily "correct" answers. Nevertheless, we've provided suggested or possible answers for many of the exercises, excluding those that result essentially in full-length paragraphs (such as those in Chapter 2) and those calling for one-paragraph or multi-paragraph essays of the students' own making.

We hope these suggested answers will help make your job easier. We know that helpless feeling an instructor occasionally has when a student asks, "How would you answer this stupid exercise?" At moments like this, your entire life may not pass before you, but certainly every doubt you ever had about becoming an English teacher does.

Besides, the suggested answers may help you decide how you want to grade homework exercises. And they can provide you with material to show your students in addition to the sample writing from the text.

The rest of this manual gives you a few tips about teaching the chapters and provides answers for the exercises.

4. Section One:
A Model for Writing

PART ONE: THE ONE-PARAGRAPH ESSAY (STAGE I)

When you begin Part One, you'll want to place it in context with the rest of the book. Explain that the tightly structured one-paragraph essay is not the final goal of good writing, but only the starting point; however, this structure need not be stifling. Although the organization is fixed, certainly the content is not, so encourage your students to be creative. This type of writing at the beginning of the book ought to be fun for everyone involved.

You also might note the advantage to your students of beginning with the one-paragraph essay: it's short. Urge them to discard their old habit of writing papers without revising them. Point out that the good habits they develop now, while the assignments are short, will make their work easier later as the assignments become longer.

Be sure you don't neglect teaching the material in the chapters. The book may seem straightforward to you—and to many of your students—but they'll pay more attention to the material you reinforce in class.

Finally, you'll want to cover at least some of the exercises in class, but supplement them with similar exercises the students haven't worked. For example, Exercises A and B for Chapter 5 ask the students to identify the transitions and reminders. You might cover these in class and then turn to another paragraph in the book (as Exercise C suggests) and ask for the transitions and reminders in it. Even better, you might bring in another paragraph, perhaps one you've written or a student's paragraph (maybe revised).

Chapter 1: Overview of the One-Paragraph Essay (Stage I)

This chapter is so short that you might want to assign Chapter 2 at the same time. You might point out, as the book says, that these paragraphs are intentionally rather skeletal. Or you might prefer to let the students assume that these paragraphs are your models for good writing. Then they will have an achievable goal: "I can write something like that!"

You may want to mention that the one-paragraph essay is rather artificial: outside the English classroom, why would anyone ever want to write such an essay? Yet the one-paragraph essay is a marvelous way for students to learn some key fundamentals of writing, since paragraphs like these occur in the middle of good essays all the time.

Exercises:

1A. TOPIC SENTENCE: Three electrical distractions waste my study time.

   SUPPORT: The humming clock reminds me of passing time.

   SUPPORT: The desk lamp buzzes, flickers, and goes out.

   SUPPORT: The computer is available for play.

   REWORDED TS: After these distractions, I'm too tired to study.

1B. TOPIC SENTENCE: Grandfather's hands mirror his strenuous working life.

   SUPPORT: Work in the sun left a permanent tan.

   SUPPORT: Splitting wood left calluses.

   SUPPORT: Carpentry left scars.

   REWORDED TS: Grandpa's hands recall his life of work.

1C. TOPIC SENTENCE: The East Wing is a showplace of modern art.

   SUPPORT: It houses collections of artists such as Picasso and Matisse.

   SUPPORT: It has a large and impressive mobile.

   SUPPORT: The building itself is a work of art.

   REWORDED TS: The East Wing is an excellent place for modern art.

1D. TOPIC SENTENCE: I like the individual freedom in Cummings' poetry.

   SUPPORT: the lack of capitalization

   SUPPORT: the content of his poems

   REWORDED TS: Cummings' poems emphasize individual freedom.

Chapter 2: Support: Examples, Statistics, Statements by Authorities

This chapter is extremely important because most students have no idea how specific good support must be. We've found that this chapter gets the students to write detailed support, particularly if you work through several of the exercises in class. You might wish to assign Exercises A, C, and D for homework, Exercise B for an in-class group exercise, and Exercises E, F, and G for homework due the next lesson.

Chapter 3: Topic Sentence

We've all considered narrowing a topic sentence so much that an electron microscope is necessary to find it. Actually, a good topic sentence for a paragraph sometimes can serve as a thesis statement for a multi-paragraph essay or, perhaps, even a research paper, though longer papers simply provide more depth of support. Keep this in mind as you discuss the exercises, especially B and C. For B we haven't always provided simple questions, and your students may write some troublesome answers for C. But a good discussion about limiting the subject and making the opinion precise won't hurt. In fact, you might want to encourage debate here; it will focus attention on the parts of the topic sentence, stimulating your students to really think about the problems of writing an effective one.

Exercises:

3A. 1. check (fact)

2. no check (opinion is "beneficial to environment")

3. check (imprecise)

4. no check (opinion is "significant drawbacks")

5. check (fact)

6. no check (the opinion is "nightmare")

7. no check ("tell the truth")

8. check (opinion is imprecise)

9. check (fact)

10. no check (opinion is "hardy")

3B. 1. Underline once: "closet."
Underline twice: "full." Circle "full."

2. Underline once: "closet."
Underline twice: "unusual design."
Circle: "fun."

3. Underline once: "chocolate."
Underline twice: "good."
Circle: "good."

4. Underline once: "fatty foods."
Underline twice: "cause health problems."

5. Underline once: "many airports."
Underline twice: "high tech features."

6. Underline once: "Today's golfers."
Underline twice: "extraordinary athletes."

7. Underline once: "Summer vacations."
Underline twice: "wonderful."
Circle: both of them.

8. Underline once: "Insecticides."
Underline twice: "harmful to human beings."

9. Underline once: "Firefighters' tactics."
Underline twice: "based on scientific research."

10. Underline once: "Soccer."
Underline twice: "great."
Circle: "great."

Chapter 4: Unity

You may wish to assign Chapters 4 and 5 for the same lesson. Exercise 4C makes a good in-class group exercise. Challenge the students to make the irrelevant sentences seem to belong in the paragraph, perhaps as a spin-off from an idea in the previous sentence.

Exercises:

4A. 1. Underline: "exhausting work."
The irrelevant sentence is 4.

2. Underline: "pioneer as a landscape painter."
The irrelevant sentence is 3.

3. Underline: "creative genius."
The irrelevant sentences are 3 and 5.

Chapter 5: Coherence

You may want to point out how coherence interrelates with unity. Have your students examine the sample incoherent paragraph at the beginning of the chapter and ask them whether they can judge the paragraph as lacking unity or coherence. What, after all, do an open window, dandruff, and smoke have to do with my roommate's being annoying? At this point, before we explain the support, we can label the paragraph's problem as appearing to lack both unity and coherence.

Actually, though, the unity is there, but incoherence conceals it. Examination of the second version of the sample paragraph, where we've added explanations of the support, shows, then, that even minimal coherence can begin to reveal unity.

Whether you treat coherence with unity or separate from it, you should notice what our chapter on coherence doesn't do. Coherence can be much more complicated than this chapter presents. Yet, if you go into pronouns, modification, logic, etc., you may overwhelm a number of your students. We've found that this chapter works quite well to teach the concept of coherence, enabling students to move smoothly from one main idea to the next.

You also should notice that we don't make a point of teaching sentence-to-sentence coherence, because we feel that we don't need to. If students learn to move smoothly from one idea to the next and to show shifts in direction of a thought, they tend to automatically learn to move smoothly from one sentence to the next.

For in-class work on coherence, you might bring in a couple of incoherent paragraphs your students have written and have the class add coherence. Or use Exercise D as the same type of in-class exercise. In addition, you could have them turn back to the sample in Chapter 1 to see if they can improve the coherence of the Boundary Waters Canoe Area paragraph. They can, of course, especially by explaining the support more fully.

Exercises F, G, H, I, and J are good out-of-class assignments; they can produce some very interesting papers. When you assign them, or some other writing topic, you might point out the checklist for the one-paragraph essay (at the end of Part Two) and tell your students to use it for this paper. If you wish to be more devious, wait until the students get ready to hand in their paragraphs and have them compare their papers to the checklist. Or have the students exchange papers and, without marking on them, compare them to the checklist. Then have the critics discuss their findings with the writers, and have the writers list on the backs of their papers what they'd change if they had the time and opportunity. This works surprisingly well.

Exercises:

5A. TOPIC SENTENCE: significant change is fear of math

      transition: for instance

    SUPPORT: book causes shiver

      transition: also

    SUPPORT: classroom arouses dread

      transition: Finally

    SUPPORT: greatest fear realized because instructor doesn't understand math

      transition: Then

    REWORDED TS: Cartesian plane has snared me in a nightmare

    CIRCLE: cold shiver (sentence 2), dread (sentence 4), cringe (sentence 5), greatest fears (sentence 6), and nightmarish (sentence 7) as reminders of fear

5B. TOPIC SENTENCE: I have learned many ways to study faster

      transition: As an example

SUPPORT: sleeping helps lead to instant memorization

transition: Another . . . developed study skills

SUPPORT: not studying during day causes increased study rate in evening

transition: But by far my most useful device

SUPPORT: writing letters during finals causes cramming

transition: Hence

REWORDED TS: developed many ways to study far faster than ever before

CIRCLE: instant memorization (sentence 2), rate . . . increase (sentence 4), sharpening my study habits (sentence 5), study . . . in only an hour and a half (sentence 6), and study far faster (sentence 7) as reminders of study faster.

5D. The city of Stockholm is among the loveliest in the world. *For example,* slum districts, prevalent in almost all large cities, are nearly nonexistent in Stockholm, having been replaced by beautiful government housing. *A visitor is also impressed by the cleanliness of the city, resulting from* the care the citizens take in picking up litter other people have dropped, as well as properly disposing of their own litter. *However, the most compelling indication of* Stockholm's *loveliness* is its unique layout: it is built on twenty-three islands. Water winding throughout the city *lends a charming, park-like quality. Not surprisingly,* the beauty of Stockholm makes it one of the most alluring cities in the world.

Chapter 6: Tips on the Writing Process

Many students have trouble writing simply because they lack an effective writing process. You probably can have a good discussion simply by asking students to share tips they have on writing.

The role of the computer also should come up. We like getting a discussion going by asking these questions:

"How many of you use a computer (or memory typewriter) for your first draft?"

"What are the advantages of using a computer for your first draft?"

Students should be able to point out these answers:

- A computer helps you revise as you draft. The writing process rarely takes you linearly through a draft.

- The computer lets you make important "mid-course corrections" that keep the paper on track.

- The computer lets you get ideas down fast. Even if you aren't a good typist, you can get ideas down quickly because you don't have to worry about mistakes.

PART TWO: THE ONE-PARAGRAPH ESSAY (STAGE II)

As with Part One, you'll want to place Part Two in context with the rest of the book and with the writing your students are accustomed to doing. The Stage II one-paragraph essay retains the simplicity of the Stage I type, but because the students now break a topic idea into its components, they move closer to the multi-paragraph essay.

Paragraph organization, of course, remains fixed, but you still can urge your students to be creative. We think you'll find, however, that students will start dealing with slightly more serious topics on their own because the requirement to break apart an idea helps lure students into choosing topics that are a little more complex.

But be aware of one problem that will start to arise. When students write the general statements that make up the subtopic sentences of the Stage II one-paragraph essay, many start cutting back on the amount of support they provide for each subtopic. The subtopic sentences, of course, add bulk to the paragraph, so students can write paragraphs as long as the Stage I type without really giving much detailed support. Since a similar problem arises as students move from the Stage II one-paragraph essay to the multi-paragraph essay and from the multi-paragraph essay to the research paper, you'll want to deal with the problem now.

You can do a couple things at this stage to ensure that students continue the detailed support they wrote for the Stage I essay. First, tell them not to worry for the moment about paragraph length—long paragraphs, for the time being, are okay. Second, reinforce the concept of providing well-developed support.

Chapter 7: Overview of the One-Paragraph Essay (Stage II)

Like the overview chapter for the Stage I one-paragraph essay, this overview chapter is short and simple, but we suggest that you not slight it. Students grasp the concept of breaking apart a topic idea more easily here with a single paragraph than they do when they write multi-paragraph essays. So the time you spend on the Stage II one-paragraph essay will make your job easier later. Instead of rushing through this overview chapter, then, we suggest you supplement it.

After you analyze the sample paragraphs in the chapter and exercises, try converting some Stage I paragraphs to Stage II types. You can go back to sample Stage I paragraphs in earlier chapters and discuss whether it's possible to add subtopic sentences to them. As the chapter points out, sometimes you can easily convert a Stage I paragraph to Stage II, but not always. Or try the same thing with Stage I paragraphs your students wrote for earlier assignments. You'll probably find that some of their Stage I paragraphs already have subtopic sentences, or at least transition sentences that announce topic shifts.

Exercises:

7A. TOPIC SENTENCE: To play water polo well, you must cheat.

   SUBTOPIC SENTENCE: Keep the ball with illegal moves.

   SUPPORT: Pushing off gives room.

   SUPPORT: Kneeing attacker in ribs saves play.

   SUBTOPIC SENTENCE: Get the ball by cheating.

   SUPPORT: Pulling opponent's leg slows him down.

   SUPPORT: Pulling his suit down stops him.

   REWORDED TS: Fortunately, water hides the cheating necessary to play water polo.

7B. TOPIC SENTENCE: Speeches take lots of work.

   SUBTOPIC SENTENCE: Hard to prepare content.

   SUPPORT: Graduation speech.

SUBTOPIC SENTENCE: Hard to prepare delivery.

SUPPORT: Gave speech to empty room.

SUPPORT: Gave speech to mirror.

SUPPORT: Gave speech to twin sister.

SUPPORT: Gave speech to parents.

REWORDED TS: So don't let people say speeches are easy.

7C. TOPIC SENTENCE: Individual freedom shows in cummings' poetry.

SUBTOPIC SENTENCE: Lack of capitalization and normal spacing.

SUPPORT: The way he writes his name.

SUBTOPIC SENTENCE: Get the ball by cheating.

SUPPORT: Content shows carefreeness of spring.

SUPPORT: Quote from a poem "Sweet spring. . . ."

REWORDED TS: So individual freedom shows in his poetry.

Chapter 8: Support: Subtopic Sentences

The lesson of this chapter carries over particularly well to longer writing assignments. Often in longer papers students organize *pieces* of the paper well but can't seem to fit the pieces together. Subtopic sentences for the Stage II one-paragraph essay (with the necessity for parallel development answering "why," "how," or "when" questions) get students accustomed to the principle of properly organizing and connecting their support ideas.

As you discuss the exercises for this chapter in class, try to get a variety of approaches for developing the topic sentences. If most students have answered "why," for example, challenge the class to try "how" or "when." Or if you have your students work an exercise in groups in class, assign different groups different approaches to the answer. Of course, some of the topics just won't work all three ways, but many will.

Remember that the checklist for the one-paragraph essay follows this chapter. You might want your students to use the checklist if you assign Exercises C through I as out-of-class writing assignments.

PART THREE: THE FIVE-PARAGRAPH ESSAY

With the full-length essay, we've come to writing more like that which your students may have been accustomed to when they began your course. But rather than trying now to connect our writing progression to what students may or may not have learned well in high school, we prefer to continue the building-block approach to organization we began with the Stage I and Stage II one-paragraph essays.

From their studies of the Stage I and Stage II one-paragraph essays, your students know how to write topic sentences and support them; they know how to break a topic idea into component ideas; and they understand unity and coherence. Studying the five-paragraph essay will show them how to adapt what they've learned to a longer, more complex piece of writing.

With Part Three we also start to make students aware of supplementing their own knowledge with facts and opinions from outside sources. You may want to allow your students to continue using invented evidence at least for some of the exercises that accompany the chapters. But you'll probably want to insist that your students stop using invented evidence on at least some out-of-class assignments. We suggest you tell them to write instead with topics and support from their own experience. And we suggest you allow them (or even urge them) to supplement their personal knowledge as necessary with knowledge from outside sources, documenting with our preliminary system. Our first suggested assignments (Chapter 12, Exercises G and H) direct students to do just this.

Finally, as with the shift from the Stage I to the Stage II one-paragraph essay, the amount of "signpost" writing (topic sentences, transitions, etc.) increases and the support that formerly was compact can become even more lengthy. Again, the danger is that students will satisfy themselves with too little and too general support. Since students tend to produce what you demand, you'll need to keep insisting on fully developed support.

Chapter 9: Overview of the Five-Paragraph Essay

You'll probably want to spend a little time in class discussing the relationship of the Stage II one-paragraph essay to the five-paragraph essay. And you'll need to explain a little about the preliminary documentation system in preparation for later work on the research paper.

Students must understand the preliminary documentation system is not complete, formal documentation; it's only a learning aid. The system does bear some resemblance to interior textual reference systems recommended by some style guides (including MLA), but our preliminary system lacks the careful documentation an interior reference system demands. Because our system is merely an aid for the moment, we've always attached to it that word "preliminary"—to keep it in its place.

Here's what the preliminary system does for your students:

- It lets them use material outside their own experience—as many will want to do at this point—to supplement their knowledge while still announcing to the reader what is theirs and what is not. That way, there's no fear of cheating.

- More important, the preliminary system eases students into the practice of using source material without the hassle, for the moment, of more formal documentation.

The real benefit of allowing preliminary documentation comes later with the research paper. Any experienced English instructor has seen that vacant, glassy-eyed stare in the faces of students who are beginning research papers. They suddenly realize they must write a paper that is longer than others they have done. They must find outside material and integrate it with their own thoughts, and they must communicate it properly.

The task can be overwhelming. They usually get it done, of course— the length, the research material, the bibliography. Yet, often under the pressure of this demanding task, they miss the part that really requires the most sophistication—integrating the source material so that it supplements their own thinking; too often research material *replaces* their thinking.

But we've found that we can move that integrating function back to the five-paragraph essay. At this point your students will still depend mostly on their own thoughts, so any outside material they use will tend to fall in its proper place, as supplemental support to their ideas. The preliminary documentation makes it possible for the students to learn to supplement their thinking, and it retains the notion of the responsibility to notify the reader that the writer is borrowing.

You, of course, have several options for dealing with preliminary documentation. You can forbid the system; students can get through Parts Three and Four using only their own experiences. You can allow students to use outside material and the preliminary documentation as the need arises in their papers. Or you can even require that they use a little outside material to get them used to the practice before they get to the special procedures for the research paper.

Chapter 10: Techniques of Layout

We consider this chapter extremely important—it lets the student's writing become realistic in appearance (instead of having unrealistically long paragraphs). At the same time, the headings and lists help students become organized. In a way, layout drives organization. That is, students who use these techniques will much more likely have clear organization than those who don't. As important, a good layout makes papers look good, look professional. Our students often take great pride in the appearance of their papers when the papers look like writing professionals in all fields of work might turn out. We've structured the book so you don't have to have your students use these techniques of layout, but we really urge you to do so.

Exercise:

From: Sam Malone

To: Diane Chambers

Subject: A proposal for a color printer and desktop publishing

We need to improve the quality of the documents and proposals we're producing in our division. To add the polish and professional look we need, I recommend we buy a color printer plus additional purchases that will let our secretaries do desktop publishing. This memo will cover

- why we need the printer
- why we need the additional purchases
- what our implementation plan will be

Why do we need a new printer?

First, I recommend we buy a color printer. The cost would be $3,400. The printer will give us two main benefits: It will add a graphics capability to both graphics work and desktop publishing. In fact, desktop publishing almost requires a color printer for a professional impact. The color printer is also fairly fast, so it will give us the crucial speed we need for rapid turnaround of final documents and proposals. It will make possible those last minute additions and changes that often improve the final presentation.

Why do we need the additional purchases?

Next, we'll need additional purchases to do desktop publishing on the printer. Here's specifically what we'll need:

- 2 copies of graphics software
- 2 training slots

What will our implementation plan be?

Once we get a color printer and the additional purchases, here's what our implementation plan will be:

- We'll add the color printer to our network so it's widely available to the staff.

- We'll install the other hardware and software on the workstations belonging to the two secretaries. One secretary is ready to do desktop publishing as soon as we get her a mouse and a graphics board. She already has software, training, and experience publishing a proposal. The other secretary needs to take the training first. That training is offered 3 weeks from now. When she's trained, we should have an excellent start for desktop publishing.

I'll be glad to talk this over with you whenever you like.

Chapter 11: Thesis Statement with Blueprint

Since the thesis statement is like a major topic sentence moved into the introduction, you'll need to say little about it. You'll probably want to discuss the blueprint with your students, and you might want to reinforce the blueprint's function: putting the blueprint ("*how* I'll tell them") after the thesis ("*what* I'll tell them") helps readers see what's coming in the rest of the essay. The combination also lets the writer—and readers—know at a glance whether the essay is likely to be unified and coherent.

You also might enlarge on the ways of combining blueprint with thesis. Here's the spectrum:

- no blueprint
- a blueprint in sentences separate from the thesis
- a blueprint in dependent clauses attached to the independent clause of the thesis
- a blueprint in phrases attached to the thesis clause
- a blueprint inside the independent clause as the limited subject of the thesis

We've chosen to teach attaching a dependent clause to the thesis because it's the easiest for beginners. But you may wish to note the other methods as well. (We've provided a variety of attachment methods in our suggested answers to the exercises.)

Exercises:

11A. 1. Important reasons for outdoor lighting are that the lights help you find doors and locks, help prevent accidents, and help prevent crime.

11A. 2. Electrical heating has advantages over natural gas in that electrical heating is cheaper, it's warmer, and it has more durable equipment.

11A. 3. Gloves are useful for warmth, decoration, and protection from injury.

11A. 4. American "hard-boiled" mysteries have many things in common: tough private eyes, uncooperative police, and lying clients.

11A. 5. Mountain vacations are ideal for getting physically fit because you can hike, climb mountains, and ride horses.

Chapter 12: Central Paragraphs

Omitting the reworded topic sentence converts a Stage I or Stage II one-paragraph essay to a central paragraph—your students will grasp this point quickly. But you'll probably need to spend time in class on the most important portions of Chapter 12: the additions to the topic sentence. Your discussion should focus on the effect these additions have on an essay's unity and coherence.

You may wish to begin by reminding your students that the basic parts of a topic sentence (limited subject and precise opinion) still give the main idea of the paragraph, just as they did with the one-paragraph essay. The need for additions arises because the writer must fit together pieces of argument located now in separate paragraphs rather than within the same paragraph. Adding a transition and a reminder of the thesis to the topic sentence of a central paragraph helps fit the paragraph into its proper place in the overall essay, thus providing unity and coherence. We suggest you spend some time in class using the sample in the chapter and the students' answers to Exercises A and B to examine these effects of altering the basic topic sentence.

Exercises:

12A. FIRST TS: Transition: First
 Reminder: requires expertise
 Main idea: compute memory

 SECOND TS: Transition: Also
 Reminder: special knowledge
 Main idea: what size hard disk

 THIRD TS: Transition: Finally
 Reminder: requires knowing about
 Main idea: type of monitor

12B. FIRST TS: Transition: For one thing
 Reminder: must constantly look
 Main idea: gauges on the dashboard

 SECOND TS: Transition: As if that's not enough . . . also
 Reminder: must pay attention to
 Main idea: the route they're traveling

 THIRD TS: Transition: And
 Reminder: have to keep a sharp lookout for
 Main idea: other traffic, including pedestrians

12C. FIRST TS: Transition: most importantly
 Reminder: Television forecasters
 Main idea: understand weather data

SECOND TS: Transition: Also
           Reminder: must know how
           Main idea: operate computer equipment

THIRD TS: Transition: Further
           Reminder: need to understand
           Main idea: proper behavior on camera

Chapter 13: Introduction

As soon as your students see that the motivator's purpose in the introduction is to "interest" the reader, some will get carried away with attracting attention. Most people are familiar with the idea of a speaker wearing a funny hat and telling a joke to begin his or her presentation. Unfortunately, students who confuse attracting interest in a topic with attracting attention will try to apply that speaker's gimmick to their essay writing. Thus, you'll probably want to remind your students to be reasonable.

A motivator should lead to the thesis, not away from it. A motivator that merely attracts attention without leading to the thesis builds expectations that the reader never will see fulfilled.

A second issue you may have to deal with is the underdeveloped introduction. The striking-statement motivator, of course, needs little length. But both the contrary-opinion and brief-story motivators, particularly the latter, profit from enough length to make them convincing and colorful.

Here's a way to attack the problem. When you review Exercise A, look for both the underdeveloped and the creative answers. Ask your students to make the underdeveloped introduction colorful; conversely, challenge students to rephrase the good introductions into bland, uninteresting ones.

Chapter 14: Conclusion

As with the motivator in the introduction, students can easily lose hold of reason when they write the clincher for the conclusion. In fact, writing an irrelevant clincher probably is easier than writing an irrelevant motivator. The temptation to digress with the clincher is there, so you'll probably want to reinforce the chapter's warning that a clincher should not present a new and unproved thesis.

Second, you may want to point out the checklist for the five-paragraph essay, which follows this chapter.

5. Section Two:
Beyond the Model Essay

PART FOUR: MORE PATTERNS OF DEVELOPMENT

Parts One to Three used a tightly structured formula to build from a simple one-paragraph essay to a five-paragraph essay. This building-block development emphasized organization, gradually expanding a simple organizational model. With Part Four, we're not discarding the model; in fact, the chapters in Part Four assume an understanding of the model five-paragraph essay. But we are shifting the emphasis slightly.

Part Four emphasizes the pattern of ideas in an essay. The chapters examine four common types of essay development:

- comparison and contrast
- cause and effect
- classification
- process

With each of these types of development, the emphasis is less on formula organization than on logical pattern within the idea; that is, support becomes as important as organization. Students should learn to align the horse and cart properly as they see that the pattern required to develop an idea is ultimately more important than the essay model. They'll learn, for example, that using three central paragraphs is a guide, not a rule, so they should lessen their dependence on the model as they increase their ability to see the pattern inherent in the development of an idea.

To reinforce this learning process for the students, we've provided the chapters in Part Four with sample essays that vary slightly from the model five-paragraph essay. After each essay, we ask the students to compare the sample essay with the abstract model. The discussions of workable variations from the model organization will help the students learn to treat the model as an aid. Our goal is not to encourage students to cast aside the model organization, but to put it in its place as a guide.

Thus, the chapters on patterns of development do not entirely break the building block flow from one-paragraph essay to research paper. With Part Five, we'll show once again the model organization, this time expanded from the five-paragraph essay to the research paper. Then students who have studied the patterns in Part Four should be able to combine support patterns with the more complex organizational pattern of the research paper.

We've designed the chapters in Part Four for concentrated study of each of four common types of essay development. Each chapter shows how to write the thesis and central paragraphs for a particular pattern of ideas and examines the pitfalls related to its development. Exercises reinforce the organizational concepts behind these idea patterns and assign full-length essays for each pattern of development.

Chapter 15: Comparison and Contrast

You'll probably want to discuss two concepts in this chapter:

- First, notice the relationship of comparison and contrast: each implies its opposite and justifies bringing items together. You might point out the similarity between acknowledging the "opposite" and using the contrary-opinion motivator your students studied in Chapter 13.

- Second, the organization of support material within central paragraphs requires careful parallelism. You might consider having your students work Exercise B together in class, with you or a student at the board as recorder.

Chapter 16: Cause and Effect

As the chapter notes, the cause-effect thesis answers "Why?" about a topic. When your students worked with subtopic sentences in exercises for Chapter 8 and the blueprint elements in Chapter 11, they probably used the "Why?" approach most often. Thus, they'll find that writing cause-effect thesis statements now is fairly easy.

Less easy is aligning topic sentences with the thesis. For this reason, Exercise A will work well for in-class discussion. If you have time, you might have each student put one answer to the exercise on the board; that way, the whole class will see and be able to discuss the outlines of a number of cause-effect papers.

Chapter 17: Classification

The two major challenges of a classification paper are related to organization and thesis. Properly identifying the classes is an organization problem; students have difficulty naming classes that are exclusive but cover their topic. They may also have trouble developing a worthwhile thesis using the classes and will settle too quickly for a thesis that merely names a number of classes.

You might try this: go over students' answers for Exercise B in class and challenge your students to develop thesis statements that use their classifications. This practice will show your students how useful classification is as a pattern of development.

Chapter 18: Process

The organization of a process paper, is, of course, crucial to its success. So look for a clean, spare appearance to the paper—look for simple clarity.

PART FIVE: THE RESEARCH PAPER

Many students fear the research paper. Sometimes because they've heard horror stories about problems graduate students encounter with theses or dissertations, they're sure the same terrors await them with an English composition research paper. Sometimes students feel the research paper is a ritual of adulthood, an impractical exercise a society of college professors dreamed up as a barrier to graduation. You can relieve your students' minds on both counts by explaining what you expect of them. They'll probably be writing a relatively short paper (something like five to ten typed pages of content) that requires the techniques of a graduate paper but not the months of drudgery or the committee reviews. And you can explain that they're learning a process of writing that relates to practical tasks (as Chapter 19 mentions), so your students see they're developing a skill they'll use both in college and later in life.

After your students accept the English composition research paper for what it is, you'll probably want to lay out the process you expect them to go through. We suggest you set up realistic goals for your students to meet at certain lessons. Make the goals landmarks that you can look at so you can check progress, ensure that the students aren't falling down on some key step, and give them the reassurance they need that they're in control of the process.

Consider discussing students' tentative topics in class so all your students can hear your comments and so the students can help each other. Keep in mind the list of possible topics at the end of Chapter 19; a topic such as "The Battle of Gettysburg" will suggest similar topics like "The Battle of the Alamo." And besides approving or disapproving topics, discuss the ways of approaching them. What caused the Battle of the Alamo? Was the defense of the Alamo a foolhardy gesture? Was the defense of the Alamo the act of an ambitious leader who should have

28

destroyed the fortress as he was ordered to? What were the results of the Battle of the Alamo? Should the Mexican army have bypassed the Alamo? And so forth. You don't have to know much about your students' topics to raise questions such as these that will help students develop thesis statements. Besides, students usually will raise questions for each other if you set the pattern of discussion.

Finally, you'll need to give your students quick feedback. Spot-check bibliography and note cards (if your students are using the traditional note-taking method). Spend a little time with each student reviewing outlines. You can even review drafts in a workshop class if you glance through for organizational points (motivator, thesis, topic sentences, etc.) instead of carefully reading the entire paper. And, of course, be alert for major blunders beginners make with research papers: choosing unlimited topics fit only for years of research, getting lost in the research so that no thesis or argument emerges, and preparing cut-and-paste papers that mindlessly string together quotations.

Chapter 19: Overview of the Research Paper

We've found that the comparison of the five-paragraph essay with the research paper helps students keep basic organization in mind as they begin their research. We suggest you emphasize the role of the short paragraphs that introduce the main idea blocks of the paper. And when you discuss organization in its abstract form, have your students identify the organizational points in the sample research paper. The sample paper doesn't follow every block of the basic diagram at the beginning of Chapter 19. Discuss whether this matters. The sample paper is short but by no means simple-minded. It deals with readily available material but approaches it with a thesis that is not widely known. And it subordinates research data to the student's own argument.

As for research paper format, the sample paper demonstrates MLA guidance—with a few exceptions:

- We added a title page because many instructors requested that we show a sample. The material facing the title page explains how to provide identifying information in the MLA format.

- We added an informative abstract, again because of instructor requests that we discuss abstracts and provide a sample with the sample research paper. MLA format does not include an abstract.

- We omitted "James 1" from the upper right corner of the first page of the paper's body because of the convention of not showing the page number on the first page of a document.

- We modified the MLA format with simple layout techniques: white space before and after the paper's title and the Works Cited page title; white space before and after headings; and lines to set off the table in the paper.

At the same time, however, we clearly marked those modifications in the comments facing the sample research paper pages, so you can have your students adhere strictly to the MLA guidance if you prefer.

If you want your students to hand in formal sentence outlines for their papers, Chapter 22 includes a sample for the research paper that appears in Chapter 19. The MLA page format is maintained in the outline sample.

Chapter 20: Finding Support

Your students may benefit from a short library tour. You can prepare one yourself, but usually library staffs are eager to show off their realms, if only because a tour eases their headaches as your students work. Many students come from towns whose libraries have little more than encyclopedias, the *Readers' Guide,* and popular magazines. Seldom are first-year students aware of the scope of material in their college library, especially the bound and automated indexes and bibliographies. Many will want to rush to the computerized list of books and the first book they find listed on their topic, so you'll probably need to help them see just how many library aids are available.

Exercises:

20B.   1.   The *Time* article is entitled "Iceman."
2.   The article appeared in the 26 October 1992 issue.
3.   The article begins on page 62.
4.   Much of the archaeological value of the site where the body was found was destroyed because no one recognized at first that the body was a scientific find rather than a recent corpse. An Austrian policeman tried to free the body from the ice with a jackhammer. Several curiosity seekers subsequently reached the site before scientists could. Even the forensic team that collected the body used an ice pickax and a ski pole to free the remains from the ice.

5. The basic library tool should be the computerized periodical indexes. If your college library has *Readers' Guide* in book or CD-ROM form, then *Readers' Guide* might be specified here. The article also is available on CD-ROM (Time Almanac 1993).

20D. 1. Ceauşescu was in the armored car for three days.
2. His wife, Elena, was with him.
3. The 30 December 1989 issue of the *New York Times* carried the article.
4. The article was in section I, page 8.
5. The *New York Times Index* provides the answers here, although the article itself also would provide the information.

20F. 1. Conant's article is "Libya's CW Gamble."
2. The United States is cited as the government leveling the charge against the Libyans.
3. The article appeared in volume 17 (2 January 1989), on page 30.
4. The computerized periodicals index should provide the information desired. *PAIS International* in automated form, on CD-ROM, or in book form also will provide the data needed.

Chapter 21: Taking and Organizing Notes

As we've mentioned, your students will benefit from discussion of topics and approaches to them. Then as they begin research, you'll need to encourage them to go slowly at first. But every class has at least one student who spends half the available time with the first book at hand. By checking bibliography cards (or copying machine products if your students use that method) early in the research process, you'll remind students to see what's actually available on their topics before they invest too much time.

You can prevent many problems if you spend some time in class looking at the similarities and differences among quotations, summaries, and paraphrases. We've designed the exercises for this chapter to focus attention on properly extracting material from sources. The exercise answers that follow for note cards are merely possible answers, of course—not the *only* answers. They can, however, serve as material for classroom discussions of quotations, summaries, and paraphrases if you reproduce them for your students.

Exercises:

21A1.

```
E77.N352                                      Th
1993

        Thomas, David Hurst, et al. The Native
        Americans: An Illustrated History.
        Ed. Betty Ballantine and Jan
        Ballantine. Atlanta: Turner, 1993.
```

21A2.

```
                                             Th1

    City of Gold

    "Coronado, gullible as all the Spanish were to
    tales of vast wealth waiting to be picked up,
    believed extravagant reports of a fabulously
    rich multistoried city near today's Arizona-New
    Mexico border. The place, called Cibola, did
    actually exist—after its own fashion. It was
    town of Zuñi pueblos."

                                         (p. 141)
```

21A3.

```
                                             Th2

    City of Gold

    Like other Spanish explorers, Coronado believed
    tales he heard of a city of enormous riches
    waiting to be conquered. The city he sought,
    Cibola, was real, but it was only a Zuñi
    pueblo, not a city of gold.

                                         (p. 141)
```

32

21A4.

```
                                                    Th3

City of Gold

The Rio Grande pueblos were not prepared to resist
the Spanish. Coronado, who like other Spanish
explorers believed the tales of a city of gold
waiting to be plundered, led a party with several
hundred Spaniards against Cibola, which turned out
to be a mere Zuñi pueblo rather than a city of
gold, so the Spanish destroyed it.

                                              (p. 141)
```

21B1.

```
                                                    Gr

Gregory, Joyce. "Lacandón Maya: Living Legacy
    in Chiapas." Native Peoples 7.3 (1994):
    38-46.
```

21B2.

```
                                                    Gr1

Descendants of the Ancient Maya

"The Lacandones are descended from Maya
survivors who fled into the rain forest
during the Spanish conquest of Yucatan and
Guatemala."

                                               (p. 38)
```

21B3.

```
                                      Gr2

  Descendants of the Ancient Maya

  The Lacandón Maya are descendants of
  ancient Maya who escaped the Spanish
  invasion by fleeing into the rain
  forest.

                              (p. 38)
```

21B4.

```
                                      Gr3

  Descendants of the Ancient Maya

  Because the Maya nation lacked both a
  supreme ruler and a governmental center,
  it fell piecemeal to the Spanish over
  some 200 years as the Spanish conquered
  the Yucatan and Guatemala. The Lacandón
  Maya of Mexico today are descendants of
  ancient Maya who fled into the rain
  forest, where they survived for
  generations by hunting, fishing, and
  raising vegetables but most of all by
  avoiding other people.

                            (pp. 38-39)
```

Chapter 22: Organizing Your Thoughts and Support

We recommend you impress on your students that outlining is the key to organization. All the successful writers we know outline to some degree, though none actually writes a formal sentence outline. Most use some sort of working outline, similar to a topic outline. For this practical reason we recommend emphasizing the topic outline.

As we explain in the text, however, topic outlines don't communicate fully. For this reason, we recommend you also discuss your students' outlines with them. That way they can explain the relationships among points, and you can watch for problems with unity and coherence.

We also recommend that you encourage your students to use headings in their papers. Headings are in wide use in writing in the "real world" beyond college; as you help your students learn to write good headings, you will be preparing them for the challenge of research writing as it is applied in the business world.

Exercise:

II. What minimum competency tests are
    A. Standardized tests of minimal skills (reading, writing, math)
    B. Connected to serious consequences (promotion or graduation)
    C. In 40 states by 1984, most connected to graduation
III. Problems the tests generate for the classroom
    A. Class time lost to teaching
        1. New Jersey—education department aided coaching
        2. Maryland—up to 15 classroom hours lost for remedial coaching on citizenship alone
    B. Narrowing of the curriculum
        1. Maryland—citizenship test on trivia
        2. Writing—grammar and punctuation rules vice writing
        3. Science—basic facts vice research process
    C. Deflection in the curriculum
        1. Emphasis on tested areas
        2. Florida 1977 survey—basic skills vice literature, language, and composition
        3. Virginia test example—parallel lines understood, perpendicular lines not
IV. How minimum competency testing holds students at risk
    A. Score improvements as simplistic measures of success
        1. Test score improvements
        2. Reaction to high stakes
    B. Tests as drivers of curriculum and teaching
        1. Determine course content and teaching methods
        2. Learning hostage to teacher evaluation
    C. Lack of connection to success in life
        1. Lack of connection of tests to earnings
        2. Connection of unemployment and lack of diploma
        3. Meaningless for college-bound students

Chapter 23: Using Borrowed Material in Your Paper

One of the hardest concepts of the research paper for most students is the relationship of source material to their own ideas. You can help by emphasizing that the outline should reflect the flow of the student's argument to convince readers of the thesis. Material from sources is subordinate, filling a support role only.

In addition, consider spending a little time in class to reinforce the difference between primary and secondary source material. In general, a student who uses primary sources will want to present healthy amounts of the original directly, but a student who uses secondary materials should reduce the amount of quotation. You might have your students look back to the sample research paper in Chapter 19; that paper, which depends on secondary sources (as your students' papers probably will), has only a few quotations. Point out how the sample paper integrates secondary source material with the writer's argument. You also could discuss why the writer chose to quote a few points and to summarize at others. Did she choose well?

Finally—and this, we think, is a key point—we've found we need to emphasize the importance of introducing source material in the paper's body. You might try pointing out that the introduction and parenthetical reference act like a frame. Everything inside the frame is connected to the source; everything outside belongs to the student.

Exercises:

23A.   1. The passage is *primary* source material. Grant, of course, is reporting on accounts in the newspapers of the day, but he is an observer of the times, and his account of the exchange with President Lincoln is firsthand information.

2. The passage fulfills all three of the basic reasons for quoting: it is worded well, is clear, and provides the words of an authority from the period discussed. Quoting Grant on his confidence in Sherman's march to the sea or quoting the Lincoln saying could be particularly effective. On the other hand, if the material used were Grant's summary of the comments of the Southern newspapers and their effect in the North, summary or paraphrase would work as well as quotation.

3. Alarmed by Southern reports that Sherman and his troops were lost and destitute on their march to the sea, Lincoln wrote Grant for reassurance. Grant wrote in his *Personal*

Memoirs that he replied to Lincoln, "with 60,000 such men as Sherman had with him, such a commanding officer as he could not be cut off in the open country" and could reach somewhere on the coast or turn north for refuge. Grant reported that Lincoln turned the reassurance into this remark: "'Grant says they are safe with such a general, and that if they cannot get out where they want to, they can crawl back by the hole they went in at'" (2:366–67).

23B. 1. This is *secondary* source material. (For discussion, ask your students what would constitute primary source material on the same topic.)

2. The entire passage is a good candidate for summary.

3. For years historians have believed that there is simply no factual foundation for the Greek stories of a race of Amazon warriors. However, an archaeological excavation opened by the Soviets in Ukraine in the 1950s produced clear evidence that Sarmatian warriors included females and that these female warriors had clearly participated in warfare. Moreover, the Sarmatian people were nomads who traded with the Greeks (Mayor and Ober 22–23), and they could have been the source of the Greek Amazon legend.

Chapter 24: Parenthetical Documentation

We have followed the *MLA Handbook* as a guide to documentation. If, like us, you grew up with the footnote system, the parenthetical documentation system will take some practice. Nevertheless, its ease and clarity will help students document effectively. You'll want to be sure your students realize that this isn't the only format guide available so they'll know where they stand when another instructor demands a different style guide. Point out that although manuals differ on minor points of format, the basic formats of style guides are very similar. Encourage your students to memorize the basic formats so they'll have little trouble adapting if someone a year or two later requires them to change manuals.

Exercises:

24A.   1. (Jameson 43–45)
　　　 2. (Roper and Jefferson 318)
　　　 3. (McDonald 2:27)
　　　 4. (Dovberg et al. 115)
　　　 5. (Backus 216–17)
　　　 6. (qtd. in Roper and Jefferson 317)
　　　 7. (Dovberg et al., Under the Gun 221)

24B.   1. Although it may be true, as McDonald asserts in *Engineers and Engineering During the American Civil War*, that "most engineering in the Civil War merely repeated the tried-and-true techniques developed over the years in European wars" (1:17), the American conflict caused the growth of a new branch of wartime engineers—railroad engineers.

　　　 2. As Franklin writes in "Railroad Engineers in the Union Army," "General Grant preferred to have his logistic tail covered by water lines of communication as he lacked confidence in the security of the railroads" (68).

Chapter 25: Works Cited

No one likes to study lists of sample bibliographic entries, but encourage your students to read the chapter carefully anyway. You can help by pointing out the more common types of entries. In addition, you might work in class on entries for a few complicated sources—for example, a book in its fourth edition that has author, editor, and translator—so students see how to use the peculiarities that sample entries illustrate and are able to fit together the pieces for such complex sources.

Exercise:

Works Cited

Adair, Linda. ʼ*People of the Desert: Hohokam Farmers and Craftsmen*.

　　Albuquerque: La Madera, 1993.

- - -. *Pots That Died: Mimbres Ceramic Arts.* Arlington: Burning Tree, 1994.

Ambler, Robert, et al. "Chaco Canyon Petroglyphs." *Chaco Canyon Archaeology.* Ed. Margaret Moulard. Baltimore: Court, 1993. 37–49.

Association of American Archaeologists. *Prehistoric Ruins in the American Southwest.* Washington: Slay, 1994.

Hardin, Clara Lee. "Potters of the Rio Grande Pueblos." *Native American Arts Today.* Nov. 1994: 46–61.

"Historic Ruins vs. Jobs—Who Wins?" Editorial. *Denver Post* 10 Oct. 94: A22.

Luckert, Wesley, and Perry S. Colton. *Societies of Prehistoric America.* 3 vols. New York: Schocken, 1992.

"New Anasazi Ruins Opened to Public." *Travel in the Southwest.* 27 May 1994: 43–45.

Tanner, Norma C. "Recent Anasazi Finds." *Journal of American Prehistory.* 3 (1994): 217–24.

6. Section Three:
Improving Your Punctuation and Expression

PART SIX: PUNCTUATION

When we first taught punctuation, our students used a standard and very popular handbook—complete but rather unwieldy as a text. We tried to help them study their assignments by going through the next day's lesson and having them put a check mark by the rules we considered especially important, the rules they seemed to violate most frequently in their own writing. Basically, we've done the same thing for your students. We've included in our test only those rules the students need the most work on. We've excluded those simple rules the students already use well, and those esoteric rules that only distract students from the important ones.

So much for philosophy. Just how do you teach punctuation? *Painstakingly.* There's no easy way, no real short cut. It takes pick-and-shovel work. Dreary as it may seem to you—and to your students—you simply have to cover all the material, all the exercises, carefully in class. There is a way to make it bearable, though—another of those group exercises. If you're fortunate and have plenty of board space, send your class to the boards and have them work in pairs (to reduce the number of answers you have to check on the spot). For Chapter 26, for example, you might ask the students to write an independent clause. Then to show them how it's done—and to set the tone for the class—write one yourself. Stay clear of "John hit the ball" and try something more bizarre: "The tiger ate the missionary," or, if you have a class clown (don't we all), "Mario showed up late for class again." Encourage your students to be imaginative, too, and the board work can be fun. If you have just a small board, send a couple of students to the board and have the others work at their desks. Then spot check answers.

You might also give objective tests every lesson. In fact, some of the exercises—the one for Chapter 26, for example—could be very good tests. You could even announce that the exercise will be an in-class test; then most of the students would learn the important material in that chapter and have a good foundation for the rest of Part VI.

Chapter 26: Definitions

26. 1. Underline once: entire sentence.

2. Underline once: entire sentence.

3. Underline once: "mow the lawn and rake the grass clippings" (*and* is CC). Underline twice: "Unless it rains tomorrow" (*Unless* is SC).

4. Underline once: "ex-President John Tyler was elected to the Confederate House of Representatives" and "the Confederates buried him with honors in Richmond" (*so* is CC). Underline twice: "Although he died before taking the new seat" (*Although* is SC) and "while the Union ignored his death" (*while* is SC).

5. Underline once: "Farmers from Massachusetts brought a 1,235-pound cheese to President Thomas Jefferson in 1802" and "the cheese was served at the White House until 1805" (*and* is CC).

6. Underline once: "Thousands of miles of wooden roads were laid in several American states in the 1840s and 1850s" (*and* is CC) and "most were replaced by gravel roads, however, when the wooden planks began to rot" (*however* is CA).

7. Underline once: entire sentence (*however* is CA).

8. Underline once: "David Rice Atchison became president of the United States for one day." Underline twice: "when Zachary Taylor delayed taking the oath of office for a day" (*when* is SC) and "because Inauguration Day fell on Sunday" (*because* is SC).

9. Underline once: "Richard Lawrence . . . fired two pistols at Andrew Jackson at point-blank range." Underline twice: "who was the first person to attempt to assassinate a US president" (*who* is RP).

10. Underline once: "both misfired." Underline twice: "Although both weapons were properly loaded" (*Although* is SC) and "although later tests proved both pistols functional" (*although* is SC; *and* is CC).

11. Underline once: "Lawrence was charged with simple assault." Underline twice: "which was a misdemeanor in those days"

41

(*which* is RP) and "because there was no legal precedent for dealing with a failed assassination attempt" (*because* is SC).

12. Underline once: "Lawrence was freed on a plea of insanity and spent the rest of his life in asylums" (*and* is CC). Underline twice: "Because the prosecutor (Washington District Attorney Francis Scott Key) agreed with the defense" (*Because* is SC) and "that Lawrence was mad" (*that* is RP).

13. Underline once: "C. W. Post marketed a wheat flake cereal as 'Elijah's Manna'" and "that name created a storm of protest from religious groups, however" (*however* is CA) and "he renamed the cereal 'Post Toasties'" (*so* is CC).

14. Underline once: entire sentence.

15. Underline once: "Fannie Farmer standardized measurements in the recipes in her first cookbook in 1896" and "to her we owe the concept of a level teaspoon."

16. Underline once: "Antonio López de Santa Anna, Mexican leader at the Alamo, brought to New York in 1869 a lump of chicle, the sap of the sapodilla tree" and "he hoped." Underline twice: "that inventor Thomas Adams could create a rubber substitute from the chicle" (*that* is RP).

17. Underline once: "Adams failed at inventing a rubber substitute from refined chicle" and "he used the chicle to create chewing gum" (*however* is CA). Underline twice: "after seeing a girl buy paraffin to chew" (*after* is SC).

18. Underline once: entire sentence (*and* is CC).

19. Underline once: "A band of travelers . . . is the subject of Chaucer's *The Canterbury Tales*." Underline twice: "who set out on a pilgrimage from an English inn" (*who* is RP).

20. Underline once: entire sentence.

21. Underline once: "Milton Hersey began building his fortune by making caramels" and "he produced chocolate formed as cigarettes and dominoes as a novelty" (*and* and *and* are CCs).

22. Underline once: "Hersey began to focus on chocolates." Underline twice: "Because chocolate would retain the impression of his name in hot weather" (*Because* is SC).

23. Underline once: "Ray Kroc was impressed by the clean, efficient, and high-volume operations in a drive-in restaurant" (*and* is CC). Underline twice: "that the McDonald brothers owned in San Bernadino, California" (*that* is RP).

24. Underline once: "Kroc persuaded the McDonald brothers to let him create a franchise of their system" and "part of the agreement, however, retained the original McDonald's name" (*however* is CA).

25. Underline once: "Kroc opened his first franchise drive-in in Des Plaines, Illinois, in 1955" and "in 5 years there were 228 franchise operations marketing some $40 million of fast-food annually."

Chapter 27: Sentence Fragment

27A. 1. (a) The Puritans fled England to seek religious freedom, but they proved intolerant of other religions in America.

   (b) The Puritans fled England to seek religious freedom; however, they proved intolerant of other religions in America.

2. (a) The term *private eye* comes from the logo of Allan Pinkerton's National Detective Agency. It showed an open eye with the words "We never sleep."

   (b) The term *private eye* comes from the logo of Allan Pinkerton's National Detective Agency; the logo shows an open eye with the words "We never sleep."

3. (a) Thomas "Boston" Corbett, of the 16th New York Cavalry, claimed to have shot John Wilkes Booth with an Army carbine; however, the autopsy showed Booth died from a pistol bullet.

   (b) Thomas "Boston" Corbett, of the 16th New York Cavalry, claimed to have shot John Wilkes Booth with an Army

carbine, but the autopsy showed Booth died from a pistol
bullet.

27B.
1.	Sentence	11.	Fragment
2.	Fragment	12.	Fragment
3.	Fragment	13.	Sentence
4.	Sentence	14.	Sentence
5.	Sentence	15.	Fragment
6.	Sentence	16.	Fragment
7.	Fragment	17.	Sentence
8.	Fragment	18.	Sentence
9.	Sentence	19.	Fragment
10.	Sentence	20.	Sentence

27C. 1. The US purchase of Alaska for $7.2 million in 1867 was not a
widely popular move; it was called "Seward's Folly" and gained
US Senate approval by only one vote.

2. The saying "buyer beware" applies to an early Sears catalog
advertisement; the ad offered a sewing machine for one dollar,
but the buyer received only a needle and thread.

3. In 1845 New York City formed a police force with 800 officers,
who soon were known as "cops" because each wore as
identification a copper star.

4. Until late in the 19th century there was no such thing as standard
time throughout the United States; the railroads, which needed
a dependable timetable for efficient operations, divided the
nation into four time zones in 1863.

5. A worldwide epidemic of influenza in 1918 killed some 27
million people, which was more than died in all of World War I.

Chapter 28: Comma Splice and Fused Sentence

28A. 1. The face of a grinning boy with big ears and one front tooth
missing was used in the 1920s to advertise a dental clinic in
Topeka, Kansas. Some 30 years later the same face became *Mad*
magazine's symbol, Alfred E. Neuman.

2. The face of a grinning boy with big ears and one front tooth
missing was used in the 1920s to advertise a dental clinic in

Topeka, Kansas; some 30 years later the same face became *Mad* magazine's symbol, Alfred E. Neuman.

3. The face of a grinning boy with big ears and one front tooth missing was used in the 1920s to advertise a dental clinic in Topeka, Kansas; indeed, some 30 years later the same face became *Mad* magazine's symbol, Alfred E. Neuman.

4. The face of a grinning boy with big ears and one front tooth missing was used in the 1920s to advertise a dental clinic in Topeka, Kansas, and some 30 years later the same face became *Mad* magazine's symbol, Alfred E. Neuman.

5. The face of a grinning boy with big ears and one front tooth missing was used in the 1920s to advertise a dental clinic in Topeka, Kansas, while some 30 years later the same face became *Mad* magazine's symbol, Alfred E. Neuman.

28B. 1. In 1924 cartoonist Harold Gray showed Capt J. M. Patterson, owner of the New York *Daily News,* a draft comic strip called "Little Orphan Otto." Because too many other comic strips starred little boys, Patterson told Gray to make the star a girl and name her Little Orphan Annie, after the popular James Whitcomb Riley poem.

2. In 1924 cartoonist Harold Gray showed Capt J. M. Patterson, owner of the New York *Daily News,* a draft comic strip called "Little Orphan Otto"; because too many other comic strips starred little boys, Patterson told Gray to make the star a girl and name her Little Orphan Annie, after the popular James Whitcomb Riley poem.

3. In 1924 cartoonist Harold Gray showed Capt J. M. Patterson, owner of the New York *Daily News,* a draft comic strip called "Little Orphan Otto"; however, because too many other comic strips starred little boys, Patterson told Gray to make the star a girl and name her Little Orphan Annie, after the popular James Whitcomb Riley poem.

4. In 1924 cartoonist Harold Gray showed Capt J. M. Patterson, owner of the New York *Daily News,* a draft comic strip called "Little Orphan Otto," but because too many other comic strips starred little boys, Patterson told Gray to make the star a girl

and name her Little Orphan Annie, after the popular James Whitcomb Riley poem.

5. When cartoonist Harold Gray showed Capt J. M. Patterson, owner of the New York *Daily News*, a draft comic strip called "Little Orphan Otto" in 1924, because too many other comic strips starred little boys, Patterson told Gray to make the star a girl and name her Little Orphan Annie, after the popular James Whitcomb Riley poem.

28C.
1. FS	8. FS	14. Correct	20. Correct
2. CS	9. CS	15. CS	21. CS
3. Correct	10. CS	16. FS	22. FS
4. CS	11. Correct	17. FS	23. Correct
5. FS	12. FS	18. FS	24. CS
6. FS	13. CS	19. CS	25. CS
7. Correct			

Chapter 29: Comma

29A. 1. Sentence B. implies that there have been other helmet laws with other provisions.

2. Sentence A. implies that not all tourists show proper respect.

3. Sentence B. implies that music has no words.

29B. 1. Andrea, which is farther north—Helsinki, Oslo, or Stockholm?

2. Joseph Stalin, who led the Soviet Union through World War II, was Time's "Man of the Year" for both 1939 and 1942.

3. *Citrus paradisi* is the name for the grapefruit tree, but whoever named it must not have been thinking of the acid pulp of the fruit.

4. As its name implies, bone china is porcelain that includes the calcium phosphate ash from burned bones.

5. In addition to its use in ceramics, bone ash is also used as a fertilizer and in cleaning and polishing compounds.

6.   *Proof* designates the strength of alcoholic liquors; for example, 100 proof liquor contains 50 percent ethyl alcohol.

7.   Atlantic City merchants began the Miss America pageant in 1921 as a gimmick to keep tourists there after Labor Day, and the first Miss America, a 16-year-old schoolgirl, won a golden statue of a mermaid.

8.   The rotund, red-cheeked man we know as Santa Claus comes from his portrayal by cartoonist Thomas Nast.

9.   Although she wanted to be known for the support she gave the feminist struggle, newspaper editor Amelia Jenks Bloomer is remembered for bloomers, the adaptation of Turkish pantaloons she popularized.

10.   Americans have been particularly disturbed by stories of clerics, who are found guilty of child abuse. (Punctuate to imply that Americans are concerned about stories about all clerics.)

11.   Americans have been particularly disturbed by stories of clerics who are found guilty of child abuse. (Punctuate to indicate that Americans are concerned about stories concerning those clerics who are found guilty of child abuse.)

12.   Samoyeds originally were breed in northern Eurasia to have a thick, long white coat; in fact, the breed's name comes from the Russian version of the Lapp words for "of Lapland."

13.   During Prohibition, which started with the 18th Amendment and ended with its repeal, it was illegal to make, sell, or transport liquor in the United States, yet drinking liquor was not against the law.

14.   As we know from books and movies about the Prohibition years, public drinking moved to speakeasies, but drinking also became popular at home, a new habit for Americans.

15.   California's wine makers produced a legal grape juice that easily became a 30-proof wine after 60 days of home fermentation.

16. Beer makers made wort, which was a half-brewed beer without alcohol; likewise, home fermentation would produce an alcoholic beer.

17. Information on making a home still was readily available in books and magazines, and the federal government even offered a pamphlet on home brewing.

18. Prohibition, Jerry, was a time when much of the American public engaged in flouting the law.

19. When Tennessee passed a law forbidding the teaching of evolution, the American Civil Liberties Union offered to defend anyone willing to test the law's prohibition of free speech.

20. John Scopes, who taught science in a Tennessee high school, was recruited to be the defendant, starting the so-called "Monkey Trial," which matched William Jennings Bryan for the prosecution against Clarence Darrow for the defense.

21. In a blow against the defense, the judge ruled that evolution was not an issue for the court; instead, the question was simply whether Scopes had broken the law by teaching evolution.

22. Scopes told *Life* magazine after the trial that he had only substituted in the biology class and that he doubted he had really taught evolution because he knew little about it.

23. The Empire State Building originally was planned to be 1,060 feet tall, only 4 feet taller than the 1,046-foot Chrysler Building, but builders added a 200-foot mooring mast for dirigibles.

24. When they realized how dangerous a dirigible mast was, the builders converted it into a tower with an observation deck.

25. Scraping the sky at 1,260 feet, the Empire State Building remained the world's tallest building for 42 years.

26. What character has been portrayed in movies by Roger Moore, George Lazenby, and David Niven?

27. Although he had achieved success as a newspaper writer, Mark Twain wanted to be published in a magazine, so he was delighted when his "Forty-Three Days in an Open Boat" appeared in *Harper's New Monthly Magazine.*

28. Unfortunately, because *Harper's* editors had trouble reading Twain's handwriting, his story appeared with the author shown as Mike Swain.

29. Unable to convict Al Capone for his more notorious crimes, the government finally imprisoned him in 1931 for income-tax evasion.

30. The *Batman* television series and movies featured the Riddler, the Joker, and the Penguin.

Chapter 30: Semicolon

30. 1. New York City Mayor Fernando Wood was a staunch supporter of the South; he proposed that the city secede, declaring itself a "free city," if the South seceded.

2. In Boston in January 1919 a steel tank filled with more than 2 million gallons of molasses popped its rivets; as the tank flew apart, the first wave of molasses was some 30 feet high.

3. The wave of molasses swept away people and animals and crushed buildings; the disaster killed 21 people and injured more than 50 others.

4. After the wave subsided, some streets were left with molasses up to 3 feet deep; for weeks people tracked molasses all over Boston, they stuck to things they touched or sat on, and the odor of molasses hung over the city.

5. Dr. James Naismith wanted a sport his students at Springfield College could play inside in the winter; he hung small goals from the gym's balcony and invented basketball.

6. The first basketball game was played in Springfield in January 1892; because the goals were peach baskets, a man had to climb a ladder after each goal to retrieve the ball.

7. This summer we plan to visit Philadelphia, for a little sight-seeing; Aunt Martha, who just moved to New York City; and Boston, where we'll look for the bar in *Cheers*.

8. Charles Willson Peale painted a tall rectangular canvas with two of his sons climbing the stairs; after he mounted the canvas in a doorway and put a real step at the bottom, the illusion was so effective that George Washington bowed a greeting to the boys.

9. Harry Nelson Pillsbury was proud of both his chess skills and his prodigious memory; he put on performances in which he played up to 22 opponents without ever seeing any of the chess boards, which meant that he had to memorize each move for each game and keep all the information in order in his head.

10. The Dust Bowl of the 1930s was centered on the area where Colorado, New Mexico, Texas, Oklahoma, and Kansas meet; in all the Dust Bowl equaled an area more than twice the size of Pennsylvania.

11. The 1920s brought prosperity to the area, and millions of acres of land were plowed and planted; however, when drought came in 1931, crop failures left nothing to hold the loose soil in place as winds swept the region.

12. In January 1933, the first great dust storm blew through the region; winds blew away an estimated 850 million tons of topsoil in just 1935.

13. Unfortunately, the natural conditions that led to the Dust Bowl still exist in the Southwest; indeed, only careful soil management and conservation keep the disaster of the 1930s from reoccurring.

14. Edith's grandchildren have moved to Tokyo, Japan; Palermo, Italy; and Cologne, Germany.

15. In November 1820, a large sperm whale rammed and sank the three-masted whaleship *Essex*; the tale brought back to Nantucket by the few survivors inspired Herman Melville's *Moby-Dick*.

16. Sequoyah was inspired by white men's written language; as a result, he created a written form of the Cherokee language even though he never learned to read or write English.

17. The family of Earl K. Long, Huey Long's younger brother and three-term governor of Louisiana, committed Earl to an asylum; when the state hospital board agreed to rule on his sanity, Earl fired the superintendent and replaced him with a friend who would declare him sane.

18. *The Prison Mirror* is the oldest continuously published prison newspaper in America; among its founders were Jim, Bob, and Cole Younger, who had been part of the Jesse James Gang.

19. Almon Brown Strowger blamed the telephone operator for diverting business from his funeral parlor to that of a competitor, so he invented the automated telephone exchange.

20. The battle between the *Monitor* and the *Merrimack* was the first battle between two ironclad ships; though their battle was inconclusive, it spelled the end of the prominence of wooden warships.

Chapter 31: Colon

31A. My vacation was a success except for one problem: extended illness.

   My vacation was an international disaster: a cold in Italy, the flu in Greece, and pneumonia in Germany.

   For one reason, I'll never forget my vacation: because I was ill in three countries.

   For one reason, I'll never forget my vacation: I was ill in three countries.

   My vacation was an international disaster: I caught a cold in Italy. When I visited Greece, I had the flu. By the time I reached Germany, I had pneumonia.

31B. The second sentence (without the colon) simply states a fact. The first sentence, however, places considerable emphasis on the information following the colon.

31C. 1. In the 14th century, Europe, Africa, and Asia were all ravaged by the same disease: the Black Plague.

2. As the two players stared at each other across the net, each communicated the same message: she was going to win.

3. As the two players stared at each other across the net, each communicated the message that she was going to win.

4. In 1215 King John granted a charter that guaranteed the English political and civil liberties: the Magna Carta.

5. As the first of the Confederate column of troops reached the Union Army command element at Appomattox, Union Major General Joshua Chamberlain gave an unusual order: he directed his soldiers to salute the Confederates as a sign of respect and peace.

6. Perhaps you know 3.14169 by its name: pi.

7. At the beginning of the American Civil War many of the uniforms varied from the standard blue and gray that would predominate later: a New York regiment in plaid kilts, regiments on both sides in colorful pantaloons and bright jackets of the French Zouaves, and even a Confederate unit with former prisoners in striped pants.

8. Many units in the war comprised recruits, and the fancy uniforms had a special purpose: their flair generated local pride and encouraged recruitment.

9. Only two countries in South America are landlocked: Bolivia and Paraguay.

10. The only countries in South America that are landlocked are Bolivia and Paraguay.

Chapter 32: Dash

32A. My vacation was a success except for one problem—extended illness.

My vacation was an international disaster—a cold in Italy, the flu in Greece, and pneumonia in Germany.

For one reason, I'll never forget my vacation—because I was ill in three countries.

For one reason, I'll never forget my vacation—I was ill in three countries.

32B. I dream of visiting Paris—for its gaiety—when schoolwork begins to pile up.

As I pulled on my gloves, I thought of Florida—of the sun mainly—and stepped outside into the snow.

I'm determined to vacation in Venice—to glide along the Grand Canal—when I can afford the trip.

I think of vacationing in Rome—visiting the Colosseum and the churches—but I usually end up at my parents' house instead.

32C. Both sentences emphasize "money"; however, the colon sets off the word formally, while the dash does so more informally, hence more personally.

32D. The dashes focus attention on the surprising chill, while the parentheses present the idea as an aside, reducing the attention given it.

32E. 1. Tourists visit Florence's Academy Gallery almost exclusively to see one work of art—Michelangelo's *David*.

2. Florence's other main galleries—the Pitti and the Uffizi—contain some of the most important art works in Europe.

3. *Geheime Staatspolizei* (or "secret state police") was shortened into an infamous contraction—Gestapo.

4. The Galapagos Islands—known for their endangered species—belong to Ecuador.

5. For the death of Sergeant Elias in Oliver Stone's *Platoon*, the music adapted from Samuel Barber's *Adagio for Strings* adds poignancy to the loss of Elias.

6. Ray Bradbury's science fiction novel about literature is named for the temperature at which paper catches fire—*Fahrenheit 451*.

7. Tourists visit Florence's Academy Gallery almost exclusively to see Michelangelo's *David*.

8. Thomas Edison—known for his exhaustive testing—said: "Genius is 1 percent inspiration and 99 percent perspiration."

9. The next time you see an ad for the low cost of fast food today, remember what a McDonald's hamburger cost in 1963—15 cents.

10. Alfred Hitchcock's *North by Northwest*—the title based on Hamlet's statement on his own madness—has insanity as an underlying theme.

Chapter 33: Apostrophe

33A.

singular possessive	plural possessive
minute's	minutes'
hobo's	hoboes'
felon's	felons'
general's	generals'
fisherman's	fishermen's
sheep's	sheep's
month's	month's
tomato's	tomatoes'
flower's	flowers'
shell's	shells'

33B. 1. Margaret Mitchell's only book was *Gone With the Wind*.

2. Tennessee Williams' *A Streetcar Named Desire* places fragile Blanche DuBois, who spends too much of her life in a fantasy world, in confrontation with Stanley Kowalski, whose life is firmly rooted in reality.

3. We've little doubt about who'll win this confrontation, but we come to realize what's lost when Blanche fails.

4. I don't know whether you'll remember, but my father promised Jenifer $3,000 if she remained unmarried until she was 23.

5. *The Crucible,* Arthur Miller's play about the Salem witch trials, has Puritan New England as its setting.

6. During a week's stay in London we went to the theater every night.

7. There's a slight buzz in one of the speakers because one of its wires is loose.

8. The eucalyptus tree's leaves make up most of the koala bear's diet.

9. Rose Greenhow, considered one of Washington's most alluring hostesses, provided the Confederates one of the Civil War's most important secrets—warning of when the Union Army was moving toward Manassas, Virginia, for the war's first battle.

10. I don't care whether that jacket is yours; just see that it's put away immediately.

11. "John Brown's Body" isn't about the John Brown who raided the federal arsenal at Harpers Ferry; instead, the song's John Brown was a sergeant in a Massachusetts volunteer regiment, whose friends made up the song to taunt him. (Note that *Harpers Ferry* does not take an apostrophe. This may cause some discussion in class, as many students will want to add an apostrophe to *Harpers.* Point out that geographic names that once depended on apostrophes today often don't have them.)

12. Karl Marx, communism's father, wasn't buried in Russia or any other of the former Soviet Union's states; you can find his grave in London.

13. For a time combination car-planes were being developed in the United States; however, they didn't fly as well as an airplane or cruise as well as an automobile, and the market's interest in them didn't last long.

14. It's been too long since we visited those relatives of yours.

15. No matter how hard I've tried to keep the dog's toys in its box, the dog has tried harder to keep its toys wherever it wants.

Chapter 34: Quotation Marks

34. 1. What Keats poem contains the statement: "Beauty is truth, truth beauty"?

2. I'm particularly fond of three short stories: Stephen Crane's "The Blue Hotel," Ernest Hemingway's "The Killers," and Robert Louis Stevenson's "Markheim."

3. In "The Blue Hotel," the Swede, who sees everyone's actions as if they were occurring in a dime novel of the Old West, says to the men playing cards, "Oh, I see you are all against me."

4. The cowboy cries out in reply, "say, what are you gittin' at, hey?"

5. Why does the Swede jump up and shout, "I don't want to fight!"?

6. Why does the cowboy reply, "Well, who the hell thought you did?"

7. Why does the cowboy later say of the Swede, "It's my opinion . . . he's some kind of a Dutchman"?

8. In "The Killers" two gangsters arrive in the diner in Summit where Nick Adams is eating; they've come to kill Ole Anderson, who usually eats dinner at the diner.

9. George, the manager, asks, "What are you going to kill Ole Anderson for? What did he ever do to you?"

10. One of the gangsters, Max, replies, "He never had a chance to do anything to us. He never even seen us."

11. The other gangster, Al, adds, "And he's only going to see us once."

12. When George again asks why the two intend to kill Ole Anderson, Max answers, "We're killing him for a friend. Just to oblige a friend, bright boy."

13. After the gangsters leave the diner, Nick goes to warn Ole Anderson, who lies listlessly in bed; Ole's response to the warning is, "There ain't anything to do."

14. Why does Ole roll toward the wall and say, "The only thing is . . . I just can't make up my mind to go out"?

15. After trying to warn Ole Anderson, Nick Adams returns to the diner and announces, "I'm going to get out of this town"; when Nick tells George that he can't stand to think about Ole just waiting in his room, George tells him, "Well . . . you better not think about it."

PART SEVEN: EXPRESSION

We consider this part of the book especially important: it's where the high school student finally becomes the college student. Unfortunately, improving expression is difficult for many students. Whereas grasping concepts of organization and support leads quickly to major improvement in students' writing, learning concepts of good expression doesn't pay off as soon for most students—they need experience. And whereas learning rules of punctuation will quickly stop silly errors in their writing, learning rules of expression still requires students to struggle with problems of judgment. Encourage your students to be patient.

As with punctuation, we urge you to cover the chapters and exercises thoroughly. Send students to the board frequently, and bring in writing samples from student papers and from outside the class whenever possible. Here are some suggestions for dealing with expression chapters in class.

Subordination and sentence variety (Chapters 35 and 36) make marked differences between the styles of the beginner and the experienced writer. For both chapters, you or your students might bring in sample writing from popular magazines like *Time*. For example, when you study subordination, give your students a well-written passage from *Time* and ask them to dilute it to grade school and early college styles. For sentence variety you can have your students butcher a good passage by rewriting the passage in simple sentences with repetitive subjects.

The chapters about parallelism, misused modifiers, subject-verb agreement, pronoun agreement, and passive voice (Chapters 37–41) all provide material for board work in class. As we suggested for the punctuation chapters, you should send students to the board in pairs. Then you and your students could discuss the answers, giving you a chance to point out the role of judgment in good expression. Even though many of the exercises for these chapters seem to be objective, some of those for parallelism, modifiers, and passive voice are quite subjective. When students have written different answers for the same exercise, challenge the students to choose which is best and explain why.

Word choice (Chapter 42) allows you to show your students that good writing needn't be stifling. Encourage students to use precise words that are imaginative but not precious. And again you have the opportunity to bring in writing by your students or by published authors. For example, you might try choosing a passage from a student paper to show how to make substantive support (a narrative example perhaps) better by improving the words. Or you can make the same points with writing you or your students choose from popular magazines.

Chapter 35: Subordination

35A. 1. a. When she was only 19, Mary Shelley wrote *Frankenstein.*
   b. Mary Shelley wrote a novel, *Frankenstein,* at the age of 19.

2. a. A small country in Central America, until 1973 Belize was called British Honduras.
   b. Called British Honduras until 1973, Belize is a small country in Central America.

3. a. After the horse won the Kentucky Derby, it was draped with a blanket of roses.
   b. The horse won the Kentucky Derby before it was draped with a blanket of roses.

4. a. The *Hindenburg,* the world's largest airship, crashed at Lakehurst, New Jersey, in 1937.
   b. The *Hindenburg*—which crashed at Lakehurst, New Jersey, in 1937—was the world's largest airship.

5. a. To win the grand prize, $64,000, on *The $64,000 Question,* Dr. Joyce Brothers answered questions on boxing.
   b. After answering questions on boxing, Dr. Joyce Brothers won the grand prize, $64,000, on *The $64,000 Question.*

35B. 1. Tired, thirsty, and hungry, Eileen finally reached the stadium, near the new mall, after riding her bike for 15 miles.

2. Although Richard Lawrence fired two pistols at Andrew Jackson at point-blank range, both pistols misfired, probably because dampness affected the powder.

3. After Clifford Berryman drew a political cartoon showing President Theodore Roosevelt refusing to shoot a cute, little bear, cuddly stuffed bears became known as "Teddy Bears."

4. Thousands of miles of wooden roads were laid in several US states in the 1840s and 1850s, but gravel roads replaced most of them when their wooden planks began to rot.

5. Even though the huge wagons that hauled borax out of Death Valley, California, in the late 1800s had eighteen mules and two horses, the idea of these teams was so popular that the product was called "twenty-mule team borax."

Chapter 36: Sentence Variety

36A. 1. Average number of words per sentence (in original): 8.6.

Possible revision: In the early 1900s, Anthony Comstock was the secretary of New York's Society for the Suppression of Vice. Comstock's excessive piousness made him appear to many Americans as a self-righteous clown. Still, he was quite effective at eliminating what he and his supporters considered lewd materials, particularly what they saw as dirty books and obscene art works. One art work Comstock attacked was painter Paul Chabas' *September Morn,* which shows a woman bathing in a lake. Even though the woman is nude, the painting is reserved by most people's standards and reveals very little. Because the painting was sure to offend Comstock, a public relations specialist decided to take advantage of the situation. He had an art dealer display a print of the painting in a shop window, and he paid some young boys to stand staring at it. Then he notified Comstock. The response was as predicted, and Chabas' painting gained national attention. The incident led to sales of millions of prints of *September Morn,* as well as dolls, calendars, and other spin-offs.

Average number of words per sentence (in this revision): 17.4.

2. Average number of words per sentence (in original): 8.7.

Possible revision: The Whiskey Rebellion, in 1794, was one of the greatest threats to the authority of the US government prior to the Civil War. The rebellion began as a test of the government's ability to collect taxes. Farmers in western Pennsylvania distilled whiskey to use up surplus corn. The liquor was cheaper to transport than corn was, and the whiskey served as currency in barter for necessities. To pay off America's war debts, in 1791 Secretary of the Treasury Alexander Hamilton imposed a tax on stills and distilled liquors. Many Pennsylvania farmers refused to pay the tax, which they compared to England's Stamp Act. By 1794 tax collectors in western Pennsylvania faced violent resistance, including frequent treatments of tar and feathers. In August 5,000 armed farmers gathered as Pittsburgh to protest the tax, and there was talk of secession. President Washington called out the militia, sending a force of 13,000, led by Major General Henry Lee, to suppress the insurrection. As the militia advanced into western Pennsylvania, resistance collapsed. The federal government had demonstrated its power.

Average number of words per sentence (in this revision): 17.6.

3. Average number of words per sentence (in original): 9.

Possible revision: Many U.S. citizens learned that in 1776 George Washington asked Betsy Ross to sew a new flag for the Continental Army. According to the story we learned, Betsy showed General Washington how to make a five-pointed star. He liked what he saw, and Betsy Ross set to work making the Stars and Stripes. Many of us even have visited the Ross house where the event took place. Moreover, we know what the resulting flag looked like. *The Spirit of '76*, a famous painting by Archibald Willard, shows the flag we're sure Betsy made. Behind two drummers and a fife player is the flag we know flew throughout the American Revolution. That flag has thirteen red and white stripes and, on a blue field in the upper left corner, thirteen white five-pointed stars in a circle. How ironic, then, that none of these "facts" is true. Although records show that Betsy Ross made flags for the Pennsylvania Navy, there is no real evidence for the Washington-Ross story. In 1870, Betsy's grandson told the tale, which he said he had learned from Betsy, to the Pennsylvania Historical Society. The legend found its way into both popular history and books. As for the flag Willard painted, there is no evidence it existed. In 1777, the Continental Congress passed a resolution that could have led to such a flag, but the flags units actually flew varied widely. Moreover, not until 1783, near the end of the war, did Washington receive the flags ordered for the Continental Army. The "history" we've learned about the Stars and Stripes, it seems, has more romance than substance.

Average number of words per sentence (in this revision): 17.

36B. Possible revision: Terrorists style themselves as separatists, anarchists, dissidents, nationalists, Marxist revolutionaries, and religious true believers. Whatever their bent, they are terrorists when they direct their violence against noncombatants. Their goal is to terrorize a wider audience than the immediate victims, thereby attempting to gain political influence. One variant is organizational terrorism. In it fall such groups as the Red Army Faction in Germany, the Red Brigades in Italy, Direct Action in France, and 17 November in Greece. These small, tightly knit, politically homogenous groups cannot gather popular support for their platforms, so they resort to terrorism. A second variant of terrorism is conducted within the context of ethnic separatist or country-wide insurgencies. In the Philippines, El Salvador, and Colombia, for example, such groups conduct paramilitary or guerrilla operations against established governments. However, they turn their attacks on the people at large to undermine a government's credibility, legitimacy, and public support.

Average number of words per sentence (in this revision): 17.

Chapter 37: Parallelism

37A. 1. He brought a set of clean linens, a towel, and a washcloth.

2. When he visited his parents, Julio wanted both to spend time with his family and to visit with old friends.

3. Greek temples for the god of medicine, Asklepios, were places not only of worship but also of healing.

4. At Christmas we like to decorate the tree, make special cookies, and sing carols.

5. Lorenzo loves hiking, climbing mountains, and especially camping in the forest.

6. The Romans constructed their baths by elevating the floors on brick pillars, enclosing the pillars and rooms to control the air circulation, and then installing furnaces to circulate hot air.

7. Edith bought a computer, a dot-matrix printer, and a popular word-processing software program.

8. Ramon never felt prepared for French class, whether he had studied the language daily or crammed several hours before class.

9. Mr. Johnston talked to a lawyer, to a judge, and to his senator about the problem.

10. We like swimming in the summer, riding horses, and cycling.

11. I didn't go to the concert because I lacked interest in it, time, and energy to go out.

12. The fountain was beautiful as the droplets spread out in the air and sparkled in the sunlight.

13. The new policy upset not only the students but also their teachers.

14. Overheated by the sun and dehydrated, I stopped running at mile seven in the July 4th road race.

15. The tomb of China's emperor Qin Shi Huangdi was protected not only by an army of over 6,000 terra-cotta soldiers but also by real drawn crossbows set to shoot intruders who set off their triggers.

16. Charles finally told his mother he wanted to go skiing, to soak in the hot tub, and always to avoid working.

17. Even though Marla was tired from jogging five miles and practicing wind sprints for twenty minutes, she was ready for a night of dancing.

18. After I revised my history paper and took a test in calculus, I still needed to study for a midterm in English.

19. Before going onto the stage and hearing the opening applause, Thea was very nervous.

20. Tossed by high waves and hammered by strong winds, the small boat seemed certain to capsize.

21. I think about Grandmother's farm when I drive in rush-hour traffic or read about crime in the streets.

22. Crane's department store is offering a special price on towels, sheets, and bedspreads.

23. Alex went to the party to enjoy the food and entertainment and to meet people who might become customers.

24. The director wanted to film scenes in the forums of ancient Rome and in the narrow, crowded streets of Naples.

25. Dennis will go to class if it neither rains nor snows.

37B. 1. Through his short stories and novels, Dashiell Hammett, creator of Sam Spade, Nick Charles, and other detectives, developed the typical "hard-boiled" detective:

- He took crime out of the drawing room of the quaint English detective story and put it into the streets.

- His dialogue captured the style and rhythm of street talk.

- His detectives were tough guys who lived by a code of honor of their own making.

2. Greek health care centers, called *Asklepieia,* offered a variety of services to the ill and infirm:

- facilities for bathing and ritual exercise

- pavilions for sleep and visits by the god of healing, Asklepios

- temples for worshipping Asklepios and for handling dogs and snakes, which were associated with Asklepios

- operating theaters where temple physicians performed surgery

3. In his war with the Celtic tribes of Gaul in 52 B.C., Julius Caesar encircled the Gauls with a field of hazards:

- The field facing the Gauls had pits with sharp stakes at the bottom—all covered with brush to hide the traps.

- A thicket of pointed branches angled toward the Gauls.

- Two trenches, one filled with water, came after the thicket.

- Finally, a steep wall with towers protected Caesar's soldiers, who could throw spears from above the attacking Gauls.

Chapter 38: Misused Modifiers

38C. 1. The audience at the gala opening of the opera was appalled when Benjamin, dressed in blue jeans and sneakers, entered the lobby.

2. After the cow was branded, the cowboy released it to run free in the pasture.

3. Because the lamb was bleating piteously, Mary allowed it to follow her to school.

4. He put the cowboy hat that he bought in Albuquerque on his head.

5. The company requests that you indicate on the enclosed card if you will accept the replacement.

6. Lorenzo seemed almost disappointed about the appointment.

7. As we drove through Yellowstone, the bears came right up to the car.

8. After the soup reaches a rolling boil, the cook can skim the fat from the surface.

9. He was a child only a mother could love.

10. When I opened the draperies, the snow had drifted halfway up the window.

11. When the tank is completely empty, the technician should refill it.

12. A woman driving a half-ton pickup and wearing a wide-brimmed hat bought the horse that won the show.

13. When the chicken is cooked, pepper should be sprinkled on it.

14. The coach told him to run wind sprints frequently. (OR The coach frequently told him to run wind sprints.)

15. Holding flowers, the boy with a shy smile approached his date.

16. With its mane flying in the wind, the horse jumped the fence.

17. To ensure they arrive on time, mail the cards by the first day of December.

18. The master of ceremonies announced the clown, who was adjusting his large, red nose.

19. The mortician figured that he had embalmed very nearly 1,200 bodies.

20. Arriving at the campground, the weary travelers rented a campsite.

21. Who is the woman in the business suit who told you how to find the studio?

22. Wearing a raincoat, a girl with a Girl Scout uniform was standing outside the supermarket selling cookies in the rain.

23. Laurie borrowed an egg that was rotten from Alice.

24. The dog with brown ears ate the food.

Ch. 42
p. 37)

25. As the wide receiver jumped high to catch the pass, the linebacker prepared to hit his legs as soon as he touched the football.

Chapter 39: Subject-Verb Agreement

39B.					
1.	has	11.	is	21.	cause
2.	is	12.	has	22.	realize
3.	is; belong	13.	has	23.	were
4.	are	14.	are	24.	carries
5.	are	15.	are	25.	are
6.	are	16.	likes	26.	have; has
7.	want	17.	was	27.	complains
8.	are	18.	was	28.	are
9.	has	19.	was	29.	is; has
10.	like	20.	was	30.	have

Chapter 40: Pronoun Agreement

40A.					
1.	his or her	6.	his	11.	their
2.	her	7.	their	12.	his or her
3.	his	8.	himself or herself	13.	its
4.	their	9.	their	14.	their
5.	they	10.	its	15.	he or she

40B. 1. Everyone wants to see what he or she can accomplish.

2. Myrna and Tina each knew their lines but neither knew her stand-in part.

3. Neither of the girls can find her scarf.

4. Warfare and hunger savaged the people, but no one seemed able to stop them.

5. After Martin and Lars lay in the sun all day, each had badly burned his arms and legs.

6. The Chamber of Commerce is seeking workers for its festival next Friday.

7. When our tour group arrived in London, I found my luggage, but neither Jerry nor Dennis could find his suitcases.

8. Economy and service may have been the garage's ideals in the beginning, but they won't do as the slogan today.

9. Each of the workers knew his or her assignment.

10. Neither Julia nor Rosemary remembered her new hours.

40C. 1. Another of the secretaries handed in a resignation today.

2. I've always wanted to thank my teachers for their contribution to my education.

3. Each of the team members will replay the game mentally tonight.

4. One of the nurses tried to use influence to convince the hospital management to modify the visitation rules.

5. A successful corporate executive expects to work long hours.

6. Can all of you finish your work on schedule?

7. The pilot is responsible for ensuring that the aircraft is serviceable before takeoff.

8. No vice president in the company will be willing to give up a personal parking place.

9. We all think we can be the best leader.

10. Lawyers know that their summations and closing arguments are crucial for their cases.

Chapter 41: Passive Voice

41A. 1. Filmmakers like southern California because the weather is favorable, labor is cheap, and local businesses are cooperative.

2. Guests at the party blew dozens of noisemakers.

3. Some 5,000 workers will work at the new factory.

4. The processing plants are in the north.

5. When sponsors could not raise funds for the Special Olympics in our town, they canceled the event.

6. We regret to inform you that we have lost your medical records.

7. The news that a federal grand jury has indicted a politician no longer surprises us.

8. When the first stage of the building is complete, the second stage may begin.

9. The third plan is the best bargain.

10. Open wire lines offer the greatest area coverage.

11. The pencil shaft is wooden.

12. The new chief executive will deliver a welcome address tomorrow.

13. No one considered the cracks in the foundation serious until the building collapsed.

14. If you are best for the job, you will hear tomorrow.

15. A short, dark-haired man with a thin mustache left the bomb in the office building.

16. For once the police caught the rapist before he could rape again.

17. The group has several factions and fronts.

18. A dark residue remains on the cleaning rag.

19. A crowd of irate citizens voiced their opposition to the tax increase.

20. If the hook is inside the eye, the door is secure.

21. Carbon dioxide is the most common lasing medium in gas lasers.

22. Once the machine starts, you must not stop it.

23. We'll begin tomorrow if the material arrives on time.

24. A thin sheet of water on the road caused the car to hydroplane.

25. Both the executives and the workers welcomed the end of the project.

41B. 1. The plan was to expand the country's agricultural base, with priority for coffee-growing and forestry segments of the economy.

2. Until it can produce high-technology components indigenously, the nation's electronics industry will remain backward.

3. Because of corruption in government and industry, the organization of the supply system is poor.

4. Using the same pistol in each attack may be the gang's way of authenticating its responsibility.

5. Nontraditional machining processes differ from traditional cutting and grinding in higher power consumption and lower material removal rates.

Chapter 42: Word Choice

42A. 1. a. The jury agreed on the defendant's innocence.
      b. The Prize Selection Committee members were struck by the painting's conception.

2. a. The Baptist leaders scorned the *Playboy* magazine.
   b. The students hated their composition text.

3. a. My neighbor picked up the Frisbee.
   b. The detective picked up the bloody glove.

4. a. The tiger devoured the missionary.
   b. The bulldog inhaled the pet food.

5. a. The minister preached about the value of a good neighbor.
   b. The huckster shouted about the value of a good juicer.

42B. 1. awed
   2. clumsily
   3. overcrowded
   4. nervous
   5. overwrought
   6. an intriguing
   7. an outstanding
   8. famished
   9. angrily
   10. anxious

42E. 1. *Batman; The Addams Family.*
   2. A *National Geographic* survey; tenth graders; Mexico and Russia are.
   3. reruns of *I Love Lucy* and *Monday Night Football.*
   4. rap lyrics; talk shows.
   5. *The Maltese Falcon.*